GAL

CENGAGE Learning

Novels for Students, Volume 17

Project Editor: David Galens

Editorial: Anne Marie Hacht, Ira Mark Milne, Pam Revitzer, Kathy Sauer, Timothy J. Sisler, Jennifer Smith, Carol Ullmann, Maikue Vang Research: Nicodemus Ford, Sarah Genik, Tamara Nott Permissions: Shalice Shah-Caldwell

Manufacturing: Stacy Melson

Imaging and Multimedia: Dean Dauphinais, Leitha Etheridge-Sims, Mary Grimes, Lezlie Light, Luke Rademacher Product Design: Pamela A. E. Galbreath, Michael Logusz © 2003 by Gale. Gale is an imprint of The Gale group, Inc., a division of Cengage Learning Inc.

For more information, contact

The Gale Group, Inc.

27500 Drake Rd.
Farmington Hills, MI 48331–3535
Or you can visit our Internet site at
http://www.gale.com

For permission to use material from this product, submit your request via Web at http://www.gale-edit.com/permissions, or you may download our Permissions Request form and submit your request by fax or mail to: *Permissions Department*
The Gale Group, Inc.
27500 Drake Rd.
Farmington Hills, MI 48331-3535
Permissions Hotline: 248-699-8006 or 800-877-4253, ext. 8006
Fax: 248-699-8074 or 800-762-4058

Since this page cannot legibly accommodate all copyright notices, the acknowledgments constitute an extension of the copyright notice.

While every effort has been made to ensure the reliability of the information presented in this publication, The Gale Group, Inc. does not guarantee the accuracy of the data contained herein. The Gale Group, Inc. accepts no payment for listing; and inclusion in the publication of any organization, agency, institution, publication, service, or individual does not imply endorsement of the editors or publisher. Errors brought to the attention of the publisher and verified to the satisfaction of the publisher will be corrected in future editions.

ISBN 0-7876-6029-9
ISSN 1094-3552

Printed in the United States of America
10 9 8 7 6 5 4 3 2 1

The Time Machine

H. G. Wells

1895

Introduction

The Time Machine was first published in 1894 as a serial under the name *The Time Traveller* in the *National Observer*. It was brought out as a book the next year under its current name and sold more than six thousand copies in a few months. H. G. Wells was just twenty-seven years old when the story, which came to be called a "scientific romance," was published. Wells's friend, William Henley, edited the *National Observer*, and Wells became part of a group of writers called "Henley's young men." The novel's appeal lies in its attempt to fathom what will become of human beings in the distant future. By making the central character of his story a time traveler who can transport himself back and forth in time with the aid of a machine he invented, Wells is able to explore many of the themes that obsessed him, including class inequality, evolution, and the relationship between science and society. In describing the future world of the effete Eloi and the cannibalistic Morlocks and the world beyond that in which all semblance of human life has been erased, Wells illustrates what he believes may very well be the fate of humanity. The novel's enduring popularity is evident in the three films adapted from the novel and the scores of others inspired by it.

Author Biography

Born in Bromley, England, on September 21, 1866, Herbert George Wells was raised in relative poverty by his father, Joseph Wells, a failed shopkeeper turned professional cricket player, and his mother, Sarah Neal Wells, a housekeeper. Wells, however, used his circumstances as a spur rather than a crutch, reading voraciously as a child in an effort to create a better life for himself. At sixteen, Wells became a student teacher at Midhurst Grammar School and was later awarded a scholarship to the Normal School of Science in London. T. H. Huxley, who, next to Darwin, was the foremost evolutionary theorist of his day, was Wells's biology teacher, and he helped to shape Wells's thinking about humankind's past and its future. Wells taught for three years after taking a bachelor of science degree in 1890, and a few years later he began writing full-time.

His first novel, *The Time Machine*, published in 1895 and hailed as one of the first great works of science fiction, was one of Wells's most popular novels and is one of his most enduring. Its success gave him the confidence to pursue his strategy of using fiction to dramatize scientific concepts such as the fourth dimension, Darwin's theory of natural selection, and Marx's theory of class struggle. In 1896, Wells published *The Island of Dr. Moreau*, about a scientist who experiments in breeding animals with human beings. Other well-known

Wells novels include *The Invisible Man* (1897) and *The War of the Worlds* (1898), the latter of which formed the basis for Orson Welles's infamous radio broadcast on October 30, 1938. In that broadcast, which millions of listeners took seriously, Welles announced that Martians had landed on Earth.

Wells was also passionate about history and politics and developed a reputation as a reformer, joining the Fabian Society, a socialist group whose members included writer George Bernard Shaw, and running for Parliament as a Labour Party candidate. As an internationally celebrated writer, he traveled to countries such as Russia, where he met with Vladimir Lenin and Josef Stalin, and the United States, where he met with President Franklin D. Roosevelt and discussed, among other topics, the implications of *The Time Machine*. Wells was also a supporter of the League of Nations, a precursor to the United Nations, serving on its Research Committee and penning books about its aims.

One of the most prolific and wide-ranging writers of the twentieth century, Wells wrote more than one hundred books, including biology textbooks, collections of short stories and literary criticism, and studies of the world economy, British imperialism, and Russian communism. He continued writing until the end of his life. Some of his later books include *Guide to the New World: A Handbook of Constructive World Revolution* (1941); *The Outlook for Homo Sapiens* (1942); *Phoenix: A Summary of the Inescapable Conditions of World Reorganisation* (1942); *A Thesis on the*

Quality of Illusion in the Continuity of Individual Life of the Higher Metazoa, with Particular Reference to the Species Homo Sapiens (1942); *The Conquest of Time* (1942); *Crux Ansata: An Indictment of the Roman Catholic Church* (1944); and *Mind at the End of Its Tether* and *The Happy Turning: A Dream of Life* (1946). At the end of his life, Wells, who had lived through two world wars, became increasingly pessimistic about humanity's future. He died in London on August 13, 1946.

Plot Summary

Chapter 1

The Time Machine begins in the Time Traveller's home at a dinner attended by various friends and acquaintances, including the Medical Man, the Psychologist, the Very Young Man, the Provincial Mayor, Filby, and Hillyer, the narrator. As the Time Traveller describes how time is the Fourth Dimension, his guests argue with him, claiming that it cannot be a dimension because people cannot move through it as they can through space. The Time Traveller excuses himself and then returns with a machine, which, after the Psychologist pushes its small lever, disappears, allegedly into the Fourth Dimension. The Time Traveller then shows the group a larger version of the time machine and announces he plans to travel through time.

Chapter 2

A week later, Hillyer, the Medical Man, and the Psychologist meet again at the Time Traveller's house, where they are joined by three newcomers: Blank, Dash, and Chose. The group begins dinner but is interrupted by the Time Traveller, who suddenly appears, haggard, thin, and dirty. After refreshing himself and eating, the Time Traveller promises to recount his story of where he has been, asserting that he has lived eight days since four o'clock that afternoon. The men are skeptical, especially Hillyer, who says, "The fact is the Time Traveller was one of those men who were too clever to be believed."

Chapter 3

In this chapter, the Time Traveller tells his story, beginning with a description of time traveling, which he calls "excessively unpleasant." Traveling faster than a year per minute, the Time Traveller describes the disorientation he feels flying through time as seasons pass in a blur. He finally decides to land, pulling on the lever to bring his machine to a crashing halt in the middle of a hailstorm. Through the hail, the Time Traveller sees an enormous sphinx carved of white marble and huge buildings and a forest. In a frenzied panic, he rushes back to the machine from which he had been thrown, desiring to leave. Just then, a group of strange creatures approaches him. He regains his confidence, and his fear subsides when one of them, four feet tall and dressed in a purple tunic, walks up to him.

Chapter 4

It is 802,701 A.D., and the Time Traveller describes the race of small creatures as being on the intellectual level of five-year-olds. The creatures take him to a large building, where a number of them sit around and eat fruit. He learns they are vegetarian and live communally in one building, with the sexes mingling freely with each other. The Time Traveller becomes frustrated by the creatures' diminishing curiosity about his presence and his inability to communicate with them. Noting the creatures' indolence and the generally dilapidated look of the buildings, the Time Traveller speculates that the creatures evolved from the human race, growing weak because they had managed to decrease their population and to erase all "hardship and vigor" from their existence. His speculation about the creatures echoes both Karl Marx and Darwin's theories of economics and evolution respectively. At the end of the chapter, the Time Traveller signals that his guesses about the creatures are wrong.

Media Adaptations

- *The Time Machine* has been adapted into film three times. Its first adaptation was released in 1960. Directed by George Pal and starring Rod Taylor, Alan Young, and Yvette Mimieux, this version could be considered the best of the three. The second adaptation, released in 1978, was directed by Henning Schellerup and stars John Beck, Priscilla Barnes, and Andrew Duggan. The most recent adaptation, released in 2002, stars Guy Pearce and Jeremy Irons and is directed by Simon Wells. All three films are widely available in libraries and major video stores.

- In 1997, Simon & Schuster Audioworks released an audiocassette of Star Trek star Leonard Nimoy reading *The Time Traveller* as part of its Alien Voices Presents Series.

Chapter 5

In this chapter, the longest in the novel, the Time Traveller discovers that his machine is missing, and he sets about to find it, guessing that it is in the base of the White Sphinx. However, he cannot open the panel to access it, and the Eloi he asks to help him all refuse. Exploring the Thames River Valley, the Time Traveller sees deep circular wells, and he speculates they are part of a vast ventilation system. Once again, his assumption will later be proved wrong.

Wells further dramatizes Marx's and Darwin's theories, as the Time Traveller learns more about the Eloi, the creatures he is staying with and whose name he learns, and is "introduced" to the Morlocks, a hideous race of underground creatures who resemble apes, with white skin and enlarged eyes, who prey on the Eloi. The Time Traveller learns about the Eloi largely through Weena, a female he rescues from drowning, while other Eloi passively watch. Weena stays with the Time Traveller, sleeping with him at night, even though she is dreadfully afraid of the dark. He later learns her fear is related to the Morlocks, who "harvest" Eloi in the dark to eat. The Time Traveller theorizes that the two races "evolved" out of the working class and the "owning" class of Victorian England. The Morlocks were the working class and had been driven underground, where they continued to work with their machines, while the Eloi were the capitalist class, who had grown dependent on the Morlocks for everything in their lives.

Chapter 6

The Time Traveller discovers a large green building, which he refers to as the Palace of Green Porcelain. He will come back to this building later in the story. For now, he braces himself to explore the underground world of the Morlocks. Weena is too afraid to follow him into the well, but the Time Traveller continues, wending his way through a maze of underground tunnels, eventually coming across a large battery of machines on which the Morlocks are hard at work. As Morlocks come toward him, the Time Traveller scares them off with a match, but he runs out of matches just as he escapes from the underground lair.

Chapter 7

In this chapter, Weena and the Time Traveller begin their journey back to the Palace of Green Porcelain but must sleep outside on a hill because night is descending. The Time Traveller muses on the insignificance of his own existence in relation to the universe and speculates on the nature of the relationship between the Morlocks and the Eloi, concluding that the underground mutants are keeping the Eloi alive both out of habit and for meat. This disgusts him and further spurs him to find his time machine.

This chapter is significant because it marks the only time that the Time Traveller stops his narrative to provide proof of his journey, pulling out "two withered flowers" that Weena had placed in his jacket pocket and putting them on the table for others to see.

Chapter 8

The Time Traveller and Weena arrive at the

Palace of Green Porcelain, which the Time Traveller inspects, discovering that it is a vast museum containing the ruins of "latter day South Kensington," with sections for natural history, paleontology, and geology. When Weena and the Time Traveller leave the museum, the Time Traveller arms himself with a box of matches and a lever he had broken off a machine in the museum with which to defend themselves against the Morlocks.

Chapter 9

In this chapter, Weena and the Time Traveller set out for the White Sphinx, where the latter believes the time machine is being kept. The two are attacked by Morlocks, and the Time Traveller lights matches to ward them off, beating them with a mace. Weary from their fighting and travel, the two fall asleep. They awaken to see frenzied Morlocks running from a raging fire the Time Traveller had set earlier. In the confusion, the Time Traveller leaves Weena behind in the burning forest.

Chapter 10

The Time Traveller finds the bronze panels at the base of the White Sphinx open and the time machine waiting for him. He jumps inside, and the Morlocks lock the doors behind him. After fighting off some of the ape-like creatures, the Time Traveller eventually starts the machine and jets into the fourth dimension.

Chapter 11

The Time Traveller lands at a time of "abominable desolation" in which there is no trace of humanity but plenty of horrendous giant crab-like creatures and enormous centipedes scurrying about in the "inky blackness." The Time Traveller has difficulty breathing and surmises the air is thinner in the future. He travels even further into the future, thirty million years, only to find that all life has vanished, except a ghastly football-sized blob trailing tentacles against the blood-red water.

Chapter 12

The Time Traveller returns to his home and his own time, convinced that because the time machine is at the other end of the laboratory, his experience was real and not a dream. He elicits responses from his guests, all of whom remain skeptical except for Hillyer, who returns the next day for more proof. The Time Traveller tells him that he will travel to the future and return in a half hour with just such evidence. Hillyer sees the Time Traveller disappear in a blur and waits for him to return, but he does not. The story ends with Hillyer saying that it has been three years since the Time Traveller left, and he has not yet returned.

Epilogue

Hillyer speculates on where the Time Traveller might be and notes the Time Traveller's pessimistic view of human progress. Even if the future is bleak, Hillyer says, human beings must live as if it is not while retaining hope for the future. This hope is symbolized by the two flowers that Weena had given the Time Traveller and that now belong to Hillyer.

Characters

Blank

The editor of "a well-known (but unnamed) daily paper," Blank—also referred to as "the Editor"—is a "rare visitor" to the Time Traveller's home. He is skeptical when told of the experiment the week before, and when the Time Traveller appears during dinner, his clothes rumpled and dirty, he makes fun of him, asking, "Hadn't they any clothes brushes in the Future?" The Editor also disbelieves the Time Traveller after he tells his story, remarking, "What a pity it is you're not a writer of stories."

Dash

Attending the second dinner, Dash—also referred to as the Journalist—"is more interested in his own stories than those of the Time Traveller."

The Eloi

Descended from the owning classes of nineteenth-century Britain, the Eloi live in 802,701 A.D. and are small, childlike creatures who spend their days playing and lounging. Vegetarians, they sleep together in large halls as protection against the Morlocks, who prey on them at night. Although initially intrigued by the Time Traveller, they quickly lose interest in him, except for Weena, a female Eloi the Time Traveller rescues from drowning.

Filby

Filby appears in the second chapter and is described as "an argumentative person with red hair." He is a rationalist who does not believe the Time Traveller's claims. He is also not very bright. Hillyer says that if Filby had presented the time machine and explained it instead of the Time Traveller, "a pork-butcher could understand."

Hillyer

Hillyer is the narrator and the only person who believes the Time Traveller's story. The bulk of the novel is the Time Traveller's story, as told to Hillyer. However, Hillyer directly addresses readers in the first, second, and twelfth chapters, and in the epilogue. Unlike the Time Traveller, who is pessimistic about humanity's future, Hillyer maintains hope, saying that even if the Time Traveller's story is true and that humanity is doomed for extinction, "it remains for us to live as though it were not so."

Medical Man

The Medical Man, also referred to as "the Doctor," is one of three guests present at both dinners. The others are Hillyer and the Psychologist. He holds a note from the Time Traveller and a watch and suggests that the group begin dinner on time, as the Time Traveller had instructed. Although he takes the Time Traveller seriously at first, he grows skeptical, believing that the Time Traveller has tricked them with his demonstration in the first chapter.

The Morlocks

In 802,701 A.D., the Morlocks live underground running their machines. Descended from Britain's nineteenth-century working class, the ape-like creatures have large eyes, white skin, and fur, and are fearful of light and fire. They also prey upon the Eloi, whom they use as a food source. They pursue the Time Traveller through the middle of his story, but he eventually beats them off and escapes into the future in his time machine.

Provincial Mayor

The Provincial Mayor is present at the first dinner. He has never heard of the fourth dimension and, in general, does not appear to know much about science.

Psychologist

The Psychologist is present at both dinners and engages the Time Traveller when he explains his theory. He says that historians would find time travel especially useful, noting, "One might travel back and verify the accepted account of the Battle of Hastings, for instance!" The Time Traveller chooses him to pull the lever on the model in the first chapter.

Time Traveller

The Time Machine is comprised mostly of the Time Traveller's story, as told to Hillyer. A well-to-do yet socially conscious inventor and a man of science who lives in Richmond, he creates a machine that allows him to travel in the fourth dimension. He has twinkling gray eyes and a pale face that is usually flushed. Well educated in the leading theories of his day, such as evolution and communism, the Time Traveller moves quickly from observation to speculation but acknowledges when he has been wrong and rethinks his position. The Time Traveller remains excited about the future, even after he learns by traveling in the future that humankind will not survive and that all trace of life will be wiped off the face of the earth. He is also a very witty man who often makes jokes at his own expense. His humor and history of playing practical jokes on his guests is one reason his guests suspect that his story is not true. Hillyer says of him that he "had more than a touch of whim among his elements."

Very Young Man

The very young man is at the first meeting

only, participating in the discussion about time travel.

Weena

Weena is an Eloi that the Time Traveller saves from drowning when other Eloi ignore her. A source of information about the Eloi, she accompanies the Time Traveller as he searches for the time machine, and the two develop a strong bond. The night before the Time Traveller returns to the past, she dies in a fire the Time Traveller sets to ward off Morlocks.

Class Struggle

Prior to the eighteenth century in the West, a person was born into a caste and remained there until he or she died. After the eighteenth century and, with the proliferation of literacy and the standardization of currency, a class system began to emerge. More people had access to old professions, such as medicine and law, and new professions, such as writing and psychology, the latter of which are represented by the Time Traveller's guests. However, with the industrial revolution and the mass migration of rural laborers into the cities, the differences between the haves and the have-nots became more starkly visible. Wells capitalizes on the struggle between these two groups in his depiction of civilization 800,000 years in the future. When he first meets the Eloi, the Time Traveller initially believes society has evolved into a form of communism. However, as he learns more, he realizes that the class struggles of the nineteenth century have continued and are manifested in the relationship between the Eloi and the Morlocks.

Science

In the nineteenth century, science became both a tool of understanding and a means of salvation. Numerous scientific theories and inventions helped science replace religion as the primary way that human beings related to their environment. Marx's theory of labor and capital and Darwin's theory of evolution described human beings as being in a constant struggle for survival, but inventions such as electricity, the telephone, and subways promised to make the struggle easier and people's lives more manageable. *The Time Machine* capitalized on the public's hunger for technology and the promise that technology offered. However, use of the time machine did not make life easier for the Time Traveller or result in any knowledge that could change the future. Rather, the Time Traveller's experiences showed a future of doom, as his journey revealed a world in which the struggles of the 1890s were not resolved but rather exacerbated. His journeys even deeper into the future revealed a world in which humanity had been extinguished from the face of the earth.

Evolution

Evolution, a theory of life's origins and humanity's development, was a groundbreaking idea in the nineteenth century and literally changed the way that people thought about themselves and their place in the world. Biological evolution focuses on changes in a population over time. Wells helped to popularize Darwin's theory of evolution by presenting the scientific theory in a popular form, fiction. The Eloi and the Morlocks represent how human beings have genetically changed in the future as a result of their ability to adapt, or not, to their environments. The Morlocks, representing a mutation of the working class of Wells's day, are ape-like, with large eyes and white skin, features that have evolved because they live underground. They fear the light and love the darkness. Conversely, the Eloi are effete, fragile, and fearful of the dark, a result of thousands of years of not having to work to survive. They represent the owning class. Ironically, the Morlocks rule the Eloi. Wells's genius is "translating" difficult concepts such as natural selection by dramatizing them in fiction.

Topics for Further Study

- In groups, draw a timeline with pictures of the evolution of human beings, beginning with prosimians and ending with the large crab-like creatures the Time Traveller encounters towards the end of his adventure. Be sure to include the Morlocks and the Eloi. Present your timeline to the class, and discuss how your timeline of human evolution differs from that of other groups.

- Assume the Time Traveller returns after three years. Write the thirteenth chapter, speculating on the kind of evidence he presents to the narrator about his travels.

- Wells believed that the human race was destined to destroy itself. In class, discuss the possibility of Wells's belief. How might what he said more than a hundred years ago come to pass in your own life or the near future?

- In *The Time Machine*, humanity "evolved" into the Morlocks and the Eloi, each representing a class of people. In groups, discuss other possible ways humanity might evolve in the future, and report your speculations to the class.

- Write a short essay identifying a specific time in the past to which you would like to return, and present reasons for your choice.

- Mark Twain's 1889 novel *A Connecticut Yankee at King Arthur's*

Court was the first novel to deal with time travel. However, the hero of that novel has no control over his journeys through time. Compare Wells's novel with Twain's, paying particular attention to the ways in which each uses time travel to satirize popular thinking and public policies. Discuss your comparisons in class.

- Wells's novel has remained popular more than one hundred years after its initial publication. What do you think accounts for its popularity? Be specific with your responses, and discuss as a class.

- The Morlocks represent the devolution of the working class of Wells's day. Many modern and contemporary representations of working class people in film and literature represent them as heroic, yet Wells's demonizes them. In a short essay, account for this choice.

Scientific Romance

A combination of fantasy and science fiction, *The Time Machine* is an example of a subgenre known as a scientific romance. A popular genre that Wells helped to refine, science fiction's action is often set in the future and examines the relationship between the future and technology. It is also defined by the appearance of characters and setting being dramatically different from those of realistic fiction. For example, the Eloi and Morlocks could not appear in a story by Ernest Hemingway, a realist. Fantasy is also a popular genre but does not necessarily rely on scientific explanations for behavior or action. Rather, fantasy fiction explores supernatural and nonrational phenomena that may or may not exist in realistic settings. J. R. R. Tolkein's *The Lord of the Rings* is a popular example of fantasy fiction. Other scientific romances of Wells's include *The Island of Doctor Moreau* (1896), *The Invisible Man* (1897), and *The War of the Worlds* (1898).

Narrator

The narrator is a speaker through whom the author tells a story. This influences the story's point of view. Wells constructs an ingenious frame for *The Time Machine*, using, in essence, two narrators.

The first is the "true" narrator, Hillyer, who introduces the Time Traveller and the other guests present at his house in the first two chapters, and who writes the concluding words in the epilogue. The second narrator is the Time Traveller himself, who takes over the narration, beginning with the third chapter, and who disappears into the future at the end of the twelfth chapter. This narrative technique allows Wells to speculate about the future and at the same time voice his positions on topics such as politics and evolution through the voice of others and within the framework of an adventure story. This strategy makes potentially difficult ideas accessible to more readers. It also gives credibility to the Time Traveller's story, as Hillyer presents the story in the Time Traveller's own words.

Symbolism

Symbols are things or ideas that stand for other things or ideas. The relationship, however, is not one to one but one to many. Wells uses symbols to evoke ideas and emotions and to figuratively stitch together many of the story's themes. For example, the Palace of Green Porcelain, a museum containing artifacts from England of the 1890s, signifies the idea of home, civilization, and extinction—all at once—for the Time Traveller. Other major symbols are the White Sphinx, which evokes the spiritual degradation of the Eloi-Morlock society, and the time machine itself, symbolizing Victorian progress and the promise—and the danger—of technology.

Historical Context

The Time Machine had numerous incarnations, the first of which was a story called "The Chronic Argonauts," which Wells published in *Science Schools Journal* in 1888. The story achieved its final form in 1894. An adherent of evolutionary theory and a staunch advocate of women's suffrage and workers' rights, Wells was deeply influenced by his times. In the 1880s and 1890s, Britain's population was booming, roughly doubling between 1851 and 1901. The rise of industrialization was emptying the farms of residents and rural laborers, as people flocked to the cities and industrial towns to work in factories. By the turn of the century, more than eighty percent of Britain's population lived in urban areas. The shift from an agricultural to an industrial economy meant that England was now dependent on imports to feed its growing population and that the landed gentry who relied on income from renting farmland now had to find another way to make money. As a city dweller and a Progressive, Wells was sensitive to the working conditions of the factory laborer. His description of the Eloi and the Morlocks dramatizes the exploitative relationship between owners and workers in Victorian England.

Wells's time machine itself was a product of an imagination nursed on the extraordinary technological advances of his day, advances that fueled industrial development and changed the complexion of the workforce. In the 1870s, for example, both the typewriter and the telephone were invented. These inventions enabled office work to be done more efficiently, work that fell overwhelmingly to women. Other inventions that altered the daily lives and thinking of Victorians include suspension bridges, the telegraph, subway trains, steamships, buses, automobiles, and electric lights. These inventions made traveling places and moving goods less expensive and opened up vistas of opportunity for entrepreneur and worker alike. Public transportation enabled workers to live farther away from urban centers, which were becoming increasingly crowded, unsafe, and unsanitary. These inventions also sped up the pace of daily life, giving it a kind of urgency previously unknown and adding to the sense that the world was spinning out of control.

England celebrated its domestic progress in 1887 with Queen Victoria's Golden Jubilee and its world empire in 1897 with its Diamond Jubilee. By the late nineteenth century, England controlled a sizeable portion of the world's land, including India, large swaths of Africa and China, Australia, and Canada. Some were outright colonies, while others held "dominion" status. The British rationalized their imperialist policies, in part, not by claiming that their acquisitions were in the military or economic interest of the country (which they were) but by claiming it was their duty as the superior race to "civilize" primitive peoples who were incapable of governing themselves. Rudyard Kipling referred to this duty as "the white man's burden." British

Prime Minister Benjamin Disraeli used Darwin's theories to support his claims for racial superiority. However, just as Britain's empire was at its peak, it began to crumble from within, as trying to contain nationalist movements spreading throughout the colonies drained Britain economically and politically.

Critical Overview

Although it sold relatively well when first published, *The Time Machine* was not widely reviewed. When it was, reviewers often likened it to Jules Verne's adventure stories or Robert Louis Stevenson's *Dr. Jekyll and Mr. Hyde*. Over the last century, it has developed a reputation as a science fiction classic. Writers like Isaac Asimov, himself a celebrated writer of science fiction, have praised the novel, noting that Wells "had the trick ... of explaining the impossible with just the right amount of gravity ... to induce the reader to follow along joyously." V. S. Pritchett was even more effusive in his praise, claiming in his essay "The Scientific Romances," "Without question *The Time Machine* is the best piece of writing. It will take its place among the great stories of our language." Bernard Bergonzi, a Wells scholar who has introduced thousands of new readers to Wells in his books and essays, argues in his essay, "*The Time Machine*: An Ironic Myth," that the novel has more "romance" than science, and is closer to the romances of nineteenth-century American writers such as Herman Melville and Nathaniel Hawthorne than it is to the work of Verne. Robert M. Philmus examines the novel for its capacity to satirize various "present ideals." In his essay "The Logic of 'Prophecy' in *The Time Machine*," Philmus reviews a number of articles written about *The Time Machine* before concluding that the Time

Traveller's return to the future at the end of the story "reinforces the fiction's claim to integrity." Other critics focus on the novel's action and its ability to entertain. For example, Richard Hauer Costa, author of *H.G. Wells*, a study of Wells's writing and life, calls the novel "a thrilling story of cosmic adventure."

Sources

Asimov, Isaac, Introduction, in *Three Novels of the Future*, Nelson Doubleday Inc., 1979, pp. vii–xii.

Bergonzi, Bernard, "*The Time Machine*: An Ironic Myth," in *H. G. Wells: A Collection of Critical Essays*, edited by Bernard Bergonzi, Prentice-Hall Inc., 1976, pp. 39–56.

Burnett, John, *The Annals of Labour: Autobiographies of British Working Class People, 1820–1920*, Indiana University Press, 1974, p. 14.

Costa, Richard Hauer, *H. G. Wells*, Twayne Publishers, 1967, pp. 31–35.

Philmus, Robert M., "The Logic of 'Prophecy' in *Time Machine*," in *H. G. Wells: A Collection of Critical Essays*, edited by Bernard Bergonzi, Prentice Hall Inc., 1976, pp. 56–69.

Pritchett, V. S., "The Scientific Romances," in *H. G. Wells: A Collection of Critical Essays*, edited by Bernard Bergonzi, Prentice Hall Inc., 1976, pp. 32–39.

Wells, H. G., *The Time Machine and Other Stories*, Scholastic Book Services, 1963, pp. 1–124.

West, Anthony, "H. G. Wells," in *H. G. Wells: A Collection of Critical Essays*, edited by Bernard Bergonzi, Prentice Hall Inc. 1976, pp. 8–25.

Further Reading

Bergonzi, Bernard, *The Early H. G. Wells: A Study of the Scientific Romances*, Manchester University Press, 1961.

> Bergonzi played a large part in establishing Wells's reputation as a great science fiction writer, arguing that Wells's scientific romances such as *The Time Machine*, *The Island of Doctor Moreau*, *The Invisible Man*, and *The War of the Worlds* are classics of the English language.

Coren, Michael, *The Invisible Man: The Life and Liberties of H. G. Wells*, Atheneum, 1993.

> Coren explores the contradictions of Wells's life, claiming that although Wells championed women's suffrage, he was also a misogynist and that although he was sympathetic to the plight of the Jews, he held anti-Semitic views.

Huntington, John, *The Logic of Fantasy: H. G. Wells and Science Fiction*, Columbia University Press, 1982.

> Huntington examines the relationship between Wells's writing and the genre of science fiction and considers how Wells contributed to

the emerging form.

MacKenzie, Norman, and Jean MacKenzie, *The Time Traveller: Life of H. G. Wells*, Weidenfeld and Nicolson, 1973.

> The MacKenzies provide a relatively straightforward and uncontroversial account of Wells's life in this accessible biography.

CPSIA information can be obtained
at www.ICGtesting.com
Printed in the USA
BVHW090946280219
541422BV00019B/484/P

9 781375 399074